MIDNIGHT'S ANGUISH

Yasmin

INDIA • SINGAPORE • MALAYSIA

ISBN 979-8-89133-703-9

Dedicated to

The dark pitched nights and intense chaos that once brimmed within.

STAGES

MAYHEM OF THE MIND 11

WAVES OF MELANCHOLY 33

MIDNIGHT'S ANGUISH 55

WATCHING GRIEF TEACH 77

METAMORPHOSIS 113

CONTENTS

1.	Inception of Mayhem	12
2.	A Silent Fray	14
3.	Chaos It Is	16
4.	Weary Rebel	18
5.	Head Residals	20
6.	Drunk on Mayhem	22
7.	Smittens, Silhouettes and Bones	24
8.	Suppressed Acts	25
9.	Enigma	26
10.	Me in You	28
11.	Bled Footprints	30
12.	Bare Voids	34
13.	Trains in Trance	36
14.	In Search	38
15.	Demise of Love	40
16.	Off Road Letter	42
17.	A Nitch of Spark	44
18.	Stopping By	46

19. Passer Devant 48
20. Tinsel Moments 50
21. By the River I Lay 52
22. A Symphony of Anguish 56
23. Seismic Set of No Emotions 58
24. Pendulum Plays 60
25. Whispers of Shadows 62
26. Murmurs Behind the Wall 64
27. Waves of Anguish 68
28. Tears in the Moonlight 70
29. Gloom within the Room 72
30. Seeking of the Unknown 74
31. She is All We Need 138
32. Nights 140

"From the moment of my birth, the angels of anxiety, worry, and death stood at my side, followed me out when I played, followed me in the sun of springtime and in the glories of summer. They stood at my side in the evening when I closed my eyes, and intimidated me with death, hell, and eternal damnation. And I would often wake up at night and stare widely into the room: Am I in Hell?"

– Edvard Munch

MAYHEM OF THE MIND

We are all sane until insanity knocks on our minds and souls unasked. And how do we navigate this unknown trail of mayhem? We never know until we do, and until then, we hang there like a leaf surviving the harsh winds of life. The following pages unfold with lines and poetry woven during the absolute mayhem.

Inception of Mayhem

Awakening to the solemn thump upon the heart's door,
After a dreary night's shallow sleep.
Mornings draped in nothing but a mayhem lore,
And finding yourself yet again in a misery heap.

Dawn's hues slowly sweeping the room's dark embrace,
Unlatched windows inviting in the breath of fresh air.
Pillows darn wet be the only proof of yesterday's haze,
With the swollen face adding to a somber stare.

Few profound sighs with eyes tucked closed,
Contemplating the quest of this feeling so obscure.
Such ruthless chaos stirring the realms of the soul,
Revealing thus the inception of mayhem so sour.

A lingering gloom inside me hosts an unsettling bluebird
demanding attention and growing like slow decay
thereby drowning me in absolute mayhem
and shunning all that's good to come.

A Silent Fray

Heart and mind embarked on a journey afar,
Spellbound by a flame — their one coveted star.
Fate intervened with such devilish sly,
Snatching the flame, no time for goodbye.

Mind, being pragmatic, urged the heart to retreat,
Yet, the heart, struck in torment, refused and stayed put.
Thus began a war, a silent fray,
A battle, so unresolved to this very day.

But what do you do with this pang of aloofness and blues that visits you often unasked?

Chaos It Is

Dissolved in chaos,
All battles and wars within.
Veins splitting their ways out gross,
Nerval diffusion going round and akin.

Bleeding out in darkness of black,
Surrounded by no means of repair.
Yet gigantic hauntings and hallucinations as these,
Always seem to have my back.

A never-ending rhythmic pattern,
Horrendous thoughts on a silver screen.
Escapism isn't a choice on turn,
Yet sorrows go to the world unseen.

Never heavenly to die each day,
Never heavenly to die this way.
Within the head we lay,
Yet never a sojourn to stay.

Hard to digest,

Harder to understand.

Weary Rebel

Exhausted, weary and burdened I am,

By being the rebel of a person.

Marching towards the wars and scars within my chest.

With the external voices igniting a burning curse.

I perish daily in the madness's embrace,

Clans of clowns persist, won't leave a trace.

Tired of rebelling, yearning for a chance,

With a moment of silence, the highest happenstance.

But don’t you think a major part of our teenage and adulthood is lost in hazes and empty races?

HEAD RESIDALS

Never was it hard to live in my head —

Well, let me stay the same.

Within my mind were a million stories,

Portrayed in scenes with intrinsic carvings.

Too good am I at living within myself,

That I created a neverland full of goblets, wine, and bliss.

Filled with characters, lovers, and passers-by,

And lived moments of quick dramas and long thrills.

But like an iceberg that hit the ship of dreams,

My head was hit by the onset of reality.

Every seashell, every stardust, every colossal memory gathered —

Was swept away and shattered clean.

Who knew? Oh —Who knew?

Even the joy spent creating illusions had its own price.

Perhaps, always had I belonged within my head.

Perhaps, reality and its world were never my claimed elements.

But, given a choice,

I'd still pick the mirages in my head.

For, to hold onto reality is like clutching the shards of broken glass,

Compared to living within the head — forever and ever.

Therefore, let me live in my illusion unapologetically,

For the damsel in me feels distressed when it faces reality,

Let alone, myself, my mind, and heart,

And choke not me for not letting any in, for I am too tired of all.

Ever wondered why illusions hold more allure than reality?

Perhaps, it's the sense of control they offer us.

Drunk on Mayhem

It rained intense outside,
All dark and stark.
Matching the intense pain,
Within her hollow heart.

Mixed cacophonies were it,
In the dim Italian bar.
Trembles and mayhem were all she felt,
A storm within, a chaotic call.

And she drank over and over,
To fill in her horrors and hollows.
Thinking to herself of what a waste,
For having spilled her truths to the one who could care less.

Lights went off one by one,
Likewise, the mob slowly and unsteadily.
However, there she sat and sobbed on her corner seat,
Drunk more on mayhem than absinthe, a silent retreat.

Has it ever occurred to you that

each time you put someone

up a pedestal you give

them a sheer chance

to look down on you?

SMITTENS, SILHOUETTES AND BONES

Smiles, a cohort for the face of mine to thine.
Suffering, spread all within, simply mine.
Washed away a few cells, half of mind and whole heart,
Far away, far away where my hands no longer catch hold of.

Bring all halves and complete myself with the leftovers,
Take no farther, make no bother.
Smitten turned abjure has become my makeover,
To fool me is to fool a sheep, easy smother.

I carry silhouettes of mine like a tread hidden,
All poise and sunshines long far unfound.
Ask me not the scenarios and stones thrown —
Can't you see me all smittens, silhouettes, and bones?

Suppressed Acts

More the delay —

More is the paralysis.

ENIGMA

Gloss and shimmers in the hallway,

Eyes adorned with roses, yet heart of stone and dust.

Sinister you are, an enigma in your veins,

Reckless breakthrough, enticement in your brook.

Arms like a thousand carved knives,

Lips spell a sure dread.

An evil epitome in every way,

A shadow trespassing neurons, always tantalising.

Echoes of wants buried within,

For a wind like you shouldn't be coveted.

They turn hearts to domes, never lasting,

Stony cobbles would do even, but never those winds.

You don’t get to change people’s hearts

All you can do is watch their hearts change.

ME IN YOU

It's sad I meant nothing much,
To you the way you meant to me.
I walked through voids all nights searching and reminiscing,
Contemplating and cruising through my chaos.

Dawns were hard, dusks were harder,
My heart similar to that of a helpless kid.
Wandered all over and found no peace,
As you wouldn't be there no more.

I would have walked right beside,
I would have limped my way too —
But honey, all you had to do was be there,
But you never could yet my bones still chant your name.

When the distance is long enough
and gazing is all you can do at the moment
would you still watch or roll on
erasing things on your way back and forth?

Bled Footprints

Clouds hanging,

The roads, unending —

Every sight seems shallow,

Every tree, so distant, so cold.

It was a cruel shrug,

To carry a heart like that —

With so many things unsaid, so much unsettled grief,

With every step forward.

The lost cuts reopen themselves,

Giving a footprint tempest —

To those who I never bid goodbye to,

And those who bid me sudden goodbyes too.

You may not know how much you love something

unless it is too near yet you had to let go

or too far to even get a hold of.

WAVES OF MELANCHOLY

After the mayhem, there arose a profound sense of melancholy surpassing all depths of gloom. It is a battleground between chaotic battles within and clouds of sadness. You remain silent, staring at the ceiling while the collective emotions of melancholy linger in you. The subsequent pages are stitched with words while being stung by the feeling of Melancholia.

Bare Voids

Dusk falls over panes,
Letting the darkness rein.
Like an intruder depleting the soul,
My soul feels captive and cold.

Not a voice flow through,
Not a word takes flight.
In a cocoon of my own I lay,
And stay staring at this plight.

Sudden visits kill,
Sudden trauma kills,
A moment like a couple of decades spin,
And the sad melancholy sweeps within.

A place I am desperately in need,
Where nothing comes through —
No voices, no melancholy, no meaningless voids,
Just the silent nights to get me through.

At times, I catch a glimpse of empty spaces

and wonder if they reflect the mirror of my heart.

Indeed, so vacant, so void, so dim, and bitterly cold.

TRAINS IN TRANCE

Two trains met,

On the same track —

For a moment in time,

It seemed passionate —

Only to convolute into nothing,

As they were immediate yet opposite —

Thereby turning all the could be's to dust.

They exploded into pieces,

Wish the trains never met,

As now there is nothing left.

Anything rushed only ends in a deep hush

resulting in intense melancholy.

In Search

Carry me from these turbulent tides,
Relieve me of pain where sorrow resides.
From the arms of melancholy, I need a break,
Willing to pay the price for serenity's sake.

In search of peace I therefore run,
In search of tranquility beneath the sun.
In search of me I therefore run,
Looking for my land of sojourn.

We realise the value of peace

only in moments of

its deprivation.

DEMISE OF LOVE

In a room where love once danced,
Now stands frozen, filled with dark cranks.
Gone are the pink, replaced by gloom,
Dry and dark, a withering bloom.

Herons that once graced the sky,
No longer soar, no longer fly.
Winds abandon their westward song,
A symphony lost; a melody gone wrong.

Sunset hues surrender to the night,
Yet the room resists the shimmering light.
No comings, goings, an eerie hush,
Laughter's echo turned to a quiet hush.

Destiny woven in every thread,
In this room, where joy has fled.
A poignant tale of love's demise,
Captured in silence, under darkened skies.

My heart yearns for the unattainable which
remains indifferent to the call of return
from my end.

Off Road Letter

The smell of jasmine,
Alongside the white sheen of moonlight.
Autumn branches unwinding,
As the wind says goodbye.

Going past the east coastline,
There she lay —
As a rain drop about to wither,
Yet shimmering all alone.

Her feet so tender and pure,
Her face calm and serene.
Her smile a rose-tinted glass,
Yet all alone on the off roads.

So beautiful, so heavenly she looked,
And some minutes it although took,
To realise it all —
Oh, to realise it all.

That she is dead,

As the letter that lay beside said.

And the slit veins on her hands alongside —

Along the off roads.

And I thought to myself,

If only she knew, if only she knew,

That she had it all in her like everybody else,

And that she could have started anew.

There are a thousand lanterns burning in your eyes guiding the passers-by, but your soul is devoid of light and why?

A Nitch of Spark

I sat there by the shore,
Intruders none, not even the breeze.
Watched the nitches of spark that passed by,
That fumed in and out like it was meant to be.

With passion the particles sprang,
And went through motion of dances.
Only to slow down,
And turn into a nothing that could have been something.

Darkness and cold started to fall,
Making my tiny shoulders shrug.
There wasn't a known hand nor a cardigan to hold me through,
And I was left alone in that deserted land.

Beyond the elements of emotions,
There felt a strange ease to the eyes.
To watch the fire rise and flame out,
Each taking its own time.

Beautiful was everything,
Beautiful was everything.
Heart so void, mind too light,
So serene, so intact.

A voice from the bruises could I hear,
And through the heart it just said,
"This moment in time there is,
This moment is all you can have and that which exist. "

Lost in melancholy we become so consumed
within ourselves that the very innate
whispers of nature go unheard.

Stopping By

It was a rather dark Saturday,
Where souls were too few in the hall.
Whence seats were many yet empty —
Like our very little hearts.

There was a single lantern hanging,
And few flowers here and there —
And the air never entered by the doorway,
And so from the windows ajar.

Oh, it was a dark sight,
Where even sunlight denied falling forth in atoms,
And there was such a sombre fragrance flying,
And also without any essence to quiver —

Every passing day was dark and dull,
Every passing night as well.
So is every passing hour and moment clubbed,
And I know not what to do whatsoever.

When we are drunk on melancholy

everything surrounding us

feels so sombre.

Passer Devant

Save me not, savour me not,

Hold me not, shoulder me not,

Care me not, caress me not,

Wake me not, watch me not,

Define me not, direct me not,

So, all I wish is —

Walk past me, walk past me,

Like how a dead flower isn't noticed,

Like how fallen leaves are ignored,

Like how the rain drops goes unnoticed,

Like how rugged roads are unentertained.

From wanting to be found

to hiding behind the shadows,

From wanting to be something to someone

to turning someone without roots,

we are all made to grow up.

Tinsel Moments

Remember the old times?

When you asked yourself not to carry the yesterdays onto the todays,

That each day carries its own moments,

That each day is separate and is unstrung?

Yet now you see in vivid patterns,

That today is new and carries no old edges —

Yet the occurring moments be whether glad or somber,

Never make it to your memory.

In a fickle of time, in a fickle of time,

Everything gets blown apart.

Except for the remnants floating in space,

Like dark clouds containing nimbus.

Habituated replaying the bygone days

that we never really let the canvas

of our lives paint anything new.

By the River I Lay

By the river I lay,
Closing my eyes and hearing the winds pass by.
A delight they are, the surroundings outside,
Yet too melancholic it is—
Within my very heart.

A void, a sullen distress,
All found home in me somehow,
All too suddenly, all over again —
I know no more how to breathe without these.

They somehow became a huge part of mine,
Juggling in my headspace.
Heaven knows the energy spent to put them off,
Yet they never leave my hay.

Watching myself bleed in pain,
It finally dawned upon me —
Maybe it's time to stop the battle,
And let the feeling of melancholy sweep.

Might as well let melancholy in

for she doesn't seem to leave

anytime soon.

MIDNIGHT'S ANGUISH

When the clock strikes twelve, and the world buries its burdens to sleep, the anguish within me slowly implodes, making the nights feel infinitely long. You grow tired of these loops of emotions swirling through you, which makes very little sense, as every visit of theirs only adds to more torment. The lines below were written during the regular sojourn of my midnight's anguish.

A Symphony of Anguish

In the theatre of life, sorrows dance,
Never easy, emotions in a delicate trance.
Highs and lows, a nocturnal song,
Knocking, uninvited, where shadows throng.

They know the passages, heart's secret chart,
Taking command, tearing every part.
Episodes unfold, a series unique,
Each time different, emotions speak.

Such is the way, the past and present waltz,
A story of anguish, where time exalts.
In the ballet of life, a continuous spree,
Episodes unfolding, an enigmatic mystery.

The anguish that found home in you yesterday

knows all paths to the heart

unlike happiness.

SEISMIC SET OF NO EMOTIONS

I stay awake at night,

Listening to the cacophonies of my heart,

And all the chances I could have taken,

To get away from everything.

And suddenly no more emotions strike,

My body frozen rigid and frenzied.

With a tear drop toppling over,

And my eyes fixated to the ceiling.

Days with intenseness were a throb,

Illness too was perhaps.

But this phase of no feeling,

Oh, seems a seizure too.

How do you stir a heart to life?

How do you stir heart to life?

Like a motionless phantom beyond the ocean,

It stays put and lies.

Is it possible for a heart to beat

still being dead?

Pendulum Plays

Nights arrive with thoughts in tow,
A pendulum swing of yesterdays' flow.
From dusk till dawn, in quiet air,
Time unfolds, a lingering affair.

The hush of dark, a contemplative space,
Pendulum whispers of the past's embrace.
Days ahead, an uncertain song,
In the night's stillness, we journey along.

There was so much darkness in the room
that the light could barely slip
through the empty spaces.

Whispers of Shadows

Moon spilled radiance, intense and bright,
Blinded senses in its luminous light.
Now, it shifts its glow, departs the scene,
Leaving us in darkness, where you've been.

No mending sought, as if unaware,
Believing nothing broke, no need for repair.
Moon seeks new canvas, another embrace,
Not on us this time, in a different space.

Yet, in the night's silence, a truth lingers,
Moonlight memories, like ghostly fingers.
A tale of brilliance, once ours to claim,
Now, in shadows, it whispers your name.

I watched you go till I could no longer watch you.

Your fading silhouette slowly dissolved

with the shadows of the night and

I neither saw you nor dawn

since then.

Murmurs Behind the Wall

Not the voices spoken clear, but muffled whispers near,

Across the walls, elusive, yet persistently here.

They strike from afar, leaving what-ifs in the air,

Restless pondering, a huge weight in the head I bear.

It's not within, but the outward echoes I dread tight,

Muffled voices of others thinking they are advising me right.

Beneath the sheets, crying alone and being out of their sight,

Is the only escapism from their echoes and hardships they give at night.

Not any voices, but those muffled and low,

A silent torment, a relentless woe.

They stir my stillness, won't let me be,

Muffled voices haunting me in secrecy.

I don't understand why anybody has to be anybody's obstacle.

Why does it often have to be that way?

Somedays are hard; I accept. Well, most of the days, when the sun's rays are so harsh and focused on you, you feel, 'Why me, O sun?' And there are days when it's completely dark, and you wonder, cry, plead, and shout, asking the same question, 'Why me, O Moon?' Yes, the same shoutout for both too much light and darkness. Yes, a few days really pierce your heart and tear you like nothing else. Initially, you wouldn't understand what's happening to your heart. It feels empty and huge at the same time. You smile, you laugh, and then the mad and the crying period starts for you. You crawl, you roll, pull pillows towards you, and hug them tighter because of the fear of being abandoned. Then you would feel that something is wrong. The moment you want to get rid of the madness in your head, you would have become accustomed to depression. In fact, so attached that when you want to change yourself to a positive and normal person, you start to feel that you want to stay depressed, stay calm, and stay dull as if it's another enlightened and heightened stage of yours. You will start to love depression and shut down so many people from your life. You lock yourself in your mind, seal your hearts too, and then turn into an artist or a writer. Yes, you heard it right. An artist or a writer you become, and oh my dear, the solace and the feeling you get when you can feed the darkness onto paper or canvas can never be satisfied. Doesn't it absorb all of it without judging you or resisting the darkness you provide on the pure, unfilled element? That is beautiful. That is companionship, and that is love. So, darkness and depression are phases that are beautiful too if you can pick up your broken pieces, hear what it has to say, and find a way to express your depression in your own way. Be it through arts, writings, or some other way so that the world will have an idea of how to get rid of depression in your way too. Deal with depression in a way that it has to be dealt with because it's a major turning point for the soul's freedom.

Waves of Anguish

Life's play, a stage I thought,

Yet everything feels like total anguish, sought.

Glad tides dry, sad tides run by quick,

Yet sudden anguish and voidness always sticks.

Always lasts, seems so, always,

Nothing sticks through in these mazes.

Passing through shades and hard phases,

Intensity lost in cacophonies embraces.

The ability to feel nothing, it never feels right,

Nor does anguish or constant pain round the clock.

Increasing cacophonies, turning us more duffer,

These waves of distress always swirling around.

Roll back to old times where pain had meaning,

Not this relentless void, incessantly leaning.

Allow me to rewind anything but this,

A time where meaning was not dismissed.

Feelings ebb and flow for a reason and

escaping is never sufficient.

So let it be.

Tears in the Moonlight

The moon, a curious confidante in the sky,
Whispered of you, making the night of mine sigh.
Usually, I blush at its gentle inquire,
Yet this time, tears joined the lunar choir.

Moonlight witnessed emotions unfold,
In its cosmic presence, secrets it holds.
A blush turned into a tender stream for it too,
This celestial conversation ending in a sad truth.

Golden hues turned ashen grey
and here I stay having nothing
more to say.

GLOOM WITHIN THE ROOM

The room which once seemed to be filled with so much love,
Withered to nil with no more pink hues anymore.
There were no herons flying back to their homes,
And no happy winds to embrace.

The sun set and darkness started to take over,
But this room seemed unaltered.
There weren't any entering and exiting whatsoever,
And the room that was once filled with laughter and happy thoughts,
Ceased to exist like it was already destined to.

And when we go through phases,

the room seems to go

through it too.

Seeking of the Unknown

O' winds, be my guide to distant shores,

Where air whispers tales unknown, evermore.

No familiar sweat in the breeze's embrace,

A voyage to lands untouched by time's trace.

Let waves be silent, withholding any name,

No indelible echoes within my mind's frame.

To the farthest lands, on your wings I'd soar,

In the embrace of the winds, forevermore.

The moon once spilled its radiance upon us, a brilliance so intense it momentarily blinded our senses. Yet, now, the moon has shifted its glow elsewhere. Instead of illuminating our dark moments, you departed, leaving things as if no mending were required—perhaps believing nothing shattered or ever existed. Hence, the moon seeks another canvas for its luminous artistry. Certainly, not upon you and me this time.

WATCHING GRIEF TEACH

Amidst frigid nights like these, a gradual awakening stirred within me. The journey down the aisle of anguish has not been in vain but instead guided me to a realm of profound stillness. Here, I become an observant pupil, witnessing grief unveil teachings to me that I can learn nowhere else.

And suddenly the unwelcomed grief that once entered unannounced turned into comfort and solace. It stopped by and found a home in me which I felt initially felt dreadful. But now, we both dine well and discuss events at night. Who knows grief can be a good friend too if only you let it enter you and you don't drive it away. I think we should welcome emotions when they stop by — especially when they come unasked. And not to forget, grief indeed is a good one until both of you don't superimpose upon each other. I guess that is how it is — for everything and for everyone.

That which helped you to find yourself

has only eased you from naivety.

There was a familiarity in those dark alleys, dark skies, and dark roads, sanity to question and a breeze that always carries the answers to yesterday's questions — that there are no tempests in the being and everything rolls as it has to. There is something in those dark approaching nights — like a once-in-a-million loops intersecting. A beauty, a serenity but especially the answers to the maddening questions for which the approach is all known. Such a grace wise entity and a sage, silent approach it contains and there is so much to be in awe with darkness too.

In the quiet night mist, I am slowly trying

to seek solace under the beautiful

quietness of the moon.

Has there ever been a time late for a new beginning? All that is needed is decluttering the yesterdays and the pangs of illusions of tomorrow that are on the way and gently going through today on the way. There is no reason to look that back or that far. It is the now — this moment, this new habit, this new you, and this is the routine you should embrace. Cut the chaos. It is simply blinding those beautiful eyes and minds. Sip the moment and forget it. Watch out for the time. Watch out for yourself and cause this beautiful aberration for yourself. You need it. Yes, you do.

If getting ahead is the only way
to mend the brittle existence,
then why not sail forth?

But the idea of shallowness is not my arena. I preferred depths even if they were as dark as the sky at night-tide or as suffocating as a confined space. Of the many things that I cannot stand, shallowness is a heavy metaphor in my own sense. It is either the intense depth of growth or mostly nothing I look for.

Shallowness finds no haven in the depths

of a select few hearts.

You can always take it slowly and steadily. You can always dance to your own pace. You can always create values for yourself. You can always stick to the things that matter to you. You can make things happen. You can always think and act. You can always do anything and be anything as long as you let yourself to. Don't succumb to anything. You are not restrained. You aren't chained. You can always move. Don't keep yourself planted. Breathe, move, laugh and progress — all in your own way.

Discovering oneself is a gradual journey, akin to unveiling the layers of a timeless masterpiece.

I love every part of the night change. The way the breeze dances to the white moon, the way the stars align themselves to make the dark sky more exquisite, the way the Earth sleeps making the land look serene, the way everything seems to be in order except the mind, sometimes. I love every part of the night and the changes she goes through while walking up the aisles of the dawn with elegance like no other. No amount of praise can equate the splendid beauty of nights because it is beyond appreciation and perhaps that is the reason I find myself spending sleepless nights trying to fit its essence in poems but each time it turns to be futile. It is simply beyond.

But few prefer the break of the night mists over the day
for that is when they find their souls dancing
amidst the darkness and the moon.
Oh lord, the dark plunging plummeting nights.

A tender dawn would suffice — a bright blue vaulted sky with swift winds and a welcoming landscape where none intrude in your path is a typically beautiful sight to behold. With the fog heaving itself up and the distant city lights shimmering in the distance, it makes everything much more sensible, adding clarity without us trying to make things clear. It happens naturally on its own.

But you are a poor moon sitting in the gutter

and admiring the stars above

not knowing that you too belong there.

That which is great and good for others may not be the same for you. Sometimes it can be a real quick nightmare. So cut it off from your system and even if there is a small voice saying you are a lot more than what you are right now, listen to it and believe it. Always depend on yourself. Fight if that is what it takes to rip all the demons off both from within and outside. And give yourself the most time possible.

All along, it quietly lingered. Perhaps, instead of dwelling in thought, we should gaze more deeply into the treasures within.

And sometimes, you don't lose interest on your own. So, when you are made to lose interest by the outward inconsistencies, you better don't question your own. It is always fine to lose interest when you are made to lose interest — either with the outsider's consciousness or not. Either way, what gets lost is lost.

Listen but never to the point that you start developing hazes to your own voice. Listen less to the outside and more on the inside, always.

We tend to adore certain moments because we are precisely sure that they are less likely to happen again. After all, what moment is a beautiful moment if you find it happening in circles? Rarity is what makes it worth the thinking I guess - the moment you realise this moment is rare while living in that very moment that makes it all worth it.

When the beginning seems satisfying,

any number of reasons said

while it ends never satiates the soul.

Perhaps you ought to get away from those who almost convince you that you know precisely nothing of what you want out of your life. It is alright if you don't know what you want from your life yet but if you know what they offer is not what you want, isn't that a knowing too?

Remove those who constantly ask you to rush through life.

They don't know any better.

They will eat you alive.

The roses have wilted. Gaze upon them, accept, and bid adieu instead of placing them between your favourite books. Stop fooling yourself into thinking they will come back to life just because you adored them more, and that their mere presence would paint over their absence. No, it won't. So bid farewell to the roses and refrain from entwining them in the tapestry of your books, garden, or life's vicinity. Not all roses are yours, and not all your roses remain so. Every rose has its timing to stay. Respect it and let it linger. When its stay is over, don't ask it to stay. Instead, gaze at the pink sky and offer a fleeting smile.

Indeed, a thorn remains a thorn;

do not romanticise it into a rose.

So much changes that you quite don't understand why everything has to change all at once. And then one day you stand in front of it and come to terms that even the tiniest of changes is so necessary and that in a long run, it has altered so many things forever. You don't remember what it was and what it had been to you and what it meant but then all of a sudden you realise, without it there can exist no version of you. It was more of a place and you feel it when there is no place like it. Each place has its aura. No two auras can never be the same. That is the case with the places I suppose.

The things I love seem to fly fastest and furthest

and now I understand that

I needed it to know

my capacity.

It is fine if you wish to walk through watching everything that is around and beyond at your own pace, at your own will and desires. You don't have to succumb to any rush that makes your tiny blisses scatter far. You don't have to go the way they go. You can make your own way with a time precise for you. It's not worth 'your energy and time'. You just don't have to. You can have it all and watch it all. Rush takes you to places quicker but also blinds you to things that your eyes could have felt pristine. It doesn't widen your mind up — that rush. It narrows it. You don't have to just because you have to. There is no 'have to'. Don't go through if you don't want to. This is one of the many things that they have forgotten to tell us — to move forward, slowly and steadily without rushing through. Maybe they never intended to tell us and we have to unlearn to re-learn.

When the soul within turns a drab,

everything around turns one.

Awaken the light and

you see squares of spirits

and rays of sunshine around.

Build yourself from scratch. Cleanse the memories that makes no sense. Kill the things that killed you or is killing you. Go ahead and get the moon. Take a step forward. Why do you wish for the blues to last? Why are you so much at war with a good life? Why are you so stubborn trying to destroy all the atoms in you. Why are you trying to cling to the winds that never come your way? Take yourself to places that fill sunshine in your chest and make you bloom hard. Give yourself some space to kill the false being within. Don't close the doors of your soul and mind just because you are afraid of the mishaps that might come along. You aren't a coward. Keep your doors wide open and let things come and go. They transform you too. Choose growth at the end. Never grieve upon anything too hard because anything of worth will never make you grieve too much anyways. Watch the beautiful sunset, read, act, teach yourself skills, paint, grow plants, watch the stars smile, laugh and so on. There is so much more. We all need fixing. Fix your mind with right or at least healthy attitude and watch happiness just follow.

A little of mind and more of heart or a little of heart

and more of mind has never done more harm

than not using either of the two or overusing

just one in any given situation.

A blend of both hasn't created much havoc, though.

Well, see things as they are. It isn't that hard. You can make things as easy or as hard as you want. It is all in the head, as it has always been. You can make your head belong to you or you can belong to your head.

Sometimes you don’t say what you wish to say

because you know it matters no more

and not because of the lack of courage.

Darkness has always contained its own spirited brilliance. If only we dive deep into it, can we appreciate its sultriness.

I like the idea of staring far and
getting lost in deep thoughts
at nights.

METAMORPHOSIS

Having traversed every stage, isn't now the moment for metamorphosis? Slowly, I embark on the journey of self-transformation, embracing the beauty of change within caused by the outside occurrences. This last part is all about the embarkment on the journey of self-transformation, savouring the exquisite dance of change within, orchestrated by the joyful rhythms of life's happenings.

You are an individual first and only then anything to anybody. You are what you are at that moment and the next moment and moment after moment. You grow, you understand, you mature. It is solely and solely your process. Nobody has anything to do with it. You are not what they visualise in their head, you are not what they wish you to be, you are not what they hope for. You are you. You are not a tree rooted. You aren't ideal. We slowly and steadily adapt and grow like the tiny leaves that spread. You are that tiny individual leaf and then you grow and grow and grow. So, you cannot be what they wish you to be. You owe nothing to no one. You simply cannot. Rebel if needed. I think we need to rebel at times because everybody seems to have some issue with us being ourselves lately. Always telecast the authentic expression of the self. Listen less because not all who give free lessons and talks have anything to do with you. Even if it were so, it doesn't matter. Don't let them stand in your way. Remove or move.

You can always find a home within you if only you don't find ways to push yourself away. You can always add aesthetics within your soul by adding cubes of empathy and love and fewer commands. You can always feel at home if you build one for yourself within your heart. You need yourself in times of dreariness and heaviness and in joy and peace. You need yourself in all stances. Don't push yourself away.

I have finally learned to remove the rose-tinted glasses I had been wearing for good. I have learned to simply see things as they are and to not equate them to my wishful thinking. I think we should not gamble an ounce of our time imagining how people will be in the near future but learn to see them as who they are without attaching any positive notions or simply any notions. I have learned to live day by day, moment by moment, and let things slip by. But I simply can't stop appreciating the beauty of nature. When I delve into it, I can't see it for what it is. It is simply beyond everything. I couldn't stop myself getting attached and feel deeply for things as these. They simply slip into your mind like a thin air. They are exquisite, huge, serene and simply a delight to our eyes. If you find yourself in the hands of nights and nature day after day, then it is all worth it. You only gain by losing yourself in it.

Total darkness isn't a saviour.

Total light isn't sunshine.

The blend of the two makes one's cup runneth.

You need to love something — anything so completely and so fully at least once so that when it exists no more, you could see where such intense feeling can lead you. It would alter you forever. Oh, you need to love. You ought to adore something — anything so wholeheartedly at-least once so that when it exists no more, you will realise that you shouldn't adore anything to the point that it has absolute ability to wreck you entirely making the glass turn to shards. You will later find yourself drawing lines because you cannot afford to mend your soul if it breaks again no more. That is the aftermath, but the pain and bruises are indeed worth it for how else would you reform yourself without calamities like these? Sometimes, you ought to jump in with both feet and see if you can survive. Maybe that way, we might know if it was worth the jump. Without bruises, there is no self-evolution anyway. Don't you think the same too?

May they go where

they have always belonged.

The most valuable thing one can give themselves is wide exposure and time. Wide exposure helps you understand that there is so much more to life than sticking to a certain certainty. Allowing yourself some time to figure out who you are leads to living a life unrushed. Give yourself the freedom and acceptance that you would want to give those who mean something to you. We all have time to live. Nothing is more brutal than you defining and putting yourself in a narrow path. Allow yourself to start and try and you will start to understand life. Don't throw your life away because you measured yourself less.

There is nothing to rush in here
and nothing to prove.
All you have to do is figure out
and be the authentic you.

How many glitches have we to stitch to turn back to a state of surface calmness? There is no single way to reach serenity. You find yourself unbelievably lost and one day you feel your pieces are in their place. This sudden paradigm shift scares you, kills you, breaks you, tears you and and do all harm to you and then suddenly disappears like a shot in the dark. You then try to work on yourself for months together yet not a single change seems to happen. Then one day, you seem to be in the highest form of yourself where you feel rivers of joy flow in you. You wouldn't know how to explain yourself on the occurrence of this happy spin but all you know is you are at peace with yourself now and that you are safe and can breathe life at night.

The ship of self-love awaits by the shore for you.

So, step aboard and enjoy the happy islands

that await you beyond the horizon of your sight.

But there are only few things that you would genuinely like and feel liberated while doing. And when you sense it and you have this inner echo within that wishes to grow with it, thats when you use all the energy in you and let that happen and keep happening throughout. You will face it in the eyes, I guess. Your only work is to recognise it and embrace it and respect it and continue doing it. That is all it takes. That is all it will ever take.

And you find yourself blooming differently when you find your thing and put in the discipline to pursue.

It perhaps would have seemed like the right thing to shun out all forms of light and to let the darkness dance all the time. It is a plain truth that it serves as a better home for the soul undoubtedly, but I wish you no more build your inner self with plain darkness. I wish you let in some light, if not all of it. And later let it spread through. Let yourself have both light and darkness like day and night. It is not that I put forth the message that darkness disappoints you however there wouldn't be much with just darkness. It occurs to me now that it has a high chance of clipping your wings and pushing you through a narrow deep dark space. You'd keep traveling and traveling and there really wouldn't be anything to watch in your journey down. I wish you turn down the total darkness and let some light seep through. A change is needed. You don't deserve all the darkness. You shouldn't settle for it. I suppose we tend to settle for it after some time is because we no more have energy to search for tiny light crystals. But search for light as you live in darkness — little by little, little by little. All I know is that one shouldn't let darkness take a toll on them for a long time even though it feels like a perfect home within after being in it for a while. You need a blend — you sure need a blend of light and darkness and not the entire veil of darkness.

You don't need a thousand sparks to lighten up your soul.

All that is ever needed is a true powerful spark

that would change you forever.

But everything we have now is that something that we had been working hard and mad to get to. As we get to it, we regard it as nothing since we finally get to see it and feel what it is like to have it and be in it. Maybe, what we have to do is to stop by, really look into it and appreciate it for what it is and appreciate ourselves for having come this far by. Acknowledging and then stepping forth for a taller height is always worth the moment rather than considering it as nothing and something that is unworthy.

Better to go till the end than assume it is nothing
only to find out it could have been something
if only you had let it be.

The more you are wired and taught, the more you lose hold of what all you can be and what all you could have done. The more you are taught what is right and bad and the more you practice it, the more you would realise later that it is just their perspective and narrowness and what they assume wrong is not entirely wrong. Nothing is entirely wrong or right. Perhaps and always, it has always been a play of perspectives. It is just that. You would watch yourself wishing that you wouldn't have listened to them as much as you did. This is the mere truth. You just would have wished to form perspectives on your own. At least then you would have learned something along the way. You sure would have.

The more you delve, the more you realize it is a one-man journey.

Maybe that is how it has always been.

Everyone gets to know only a part of us. Only a few gain access to both our minds and hearts, and that is becoming increasingly rare. Therefore, somewhere down the line, the untold parts of us seek shelter by hiding, yet they also desire to project themselves out in the nights, at early dawns, while hearing a piece of distant music, contemplating too much, and having to say too little. This happens while watching the sunsets and sunrises too. Perhaps that is the reason we hold nature very dear.

Darling, finding our own place helps.

Trying to fit in has never done any good.

In a seemingly endless loop, I tried, failed, and repeated the cycle tirelessly. Each attempt only led to more failures, creating a sense of futility. Eventually, I grew profoundly weary, drained of both soul and energy, leaving me in a state of emptiness. Strangely, I found a silver lining in those challenging days; they prompted deep introspection. Through persistent contemplation, I sought to unravel the meaning behind my endeavours, only to discover a profound lack of intrinsic purpose. This realisation brought a peculiar sense of relief—I wasn't meant for that particular path. Embracing the failures, I acknowledged that they had, ironically, fuelled a search for meaning. This transformative journey broadened my perspective. Instead of futile attempts, I learned the value of thoughtful reflection. The lesson became clear: in moments of failure, don't merely strive harder but contemplate deeply, as the answers often reside within. All aspects of chaos and harmony coexist within the realm of self-discovery.

In the dark times, look within. There are answers already.

Ask the right questions to yourself for yourself.

You don't have to be fond of every responsibility that comes along the way or that they thrust upon you. Not everything is going to help you grow. How good is something for you when all it does is cause fatigue to your body and heart but just makes you look appealing according to the status quo? You have nothing to show others. All you ought to focus on is that inward glow and how beautifully you emerge from situations that comes upfront. It is as simple as that. It has always been that. You don't have to look appealing just in the eyes of others. The path is always within. Do it for yourself. Let not the thought of others make you do things which otherwise doesn't seem fascinating to yourself.

Just because it flows through you doesn't mean that it is easy.

Put in the necessary efforts and watch yourself shine through.

She is All We Need

The thin air hanging,
Happy and sad faces wandering.
Waves hitting the rocks at their pace,
Trees dancing to their own rhythm in full solace.
Birds finding their way back home,
Poets writing their final pieces of melancholy,
Old man capturing life in his Kodachrome,
Lovers trying to kiss under sunset,
Boys playing as merrily as ever.
Girls living in their own land,
The sky in her grey coat,
Waves in their blue blanket,
Every emotion in one place,
So surreal, so surreal —
Every day the place seems different,
Each day more wholesome,
More joyous and more of everything
And her love runneth over.
She is all we need — the sea.

Nights and the sea are the pure paradise for those who know how to embrace it.

Nights

The sky —

A beautiful opera,

The stars and moon —

Her performers,

On nights like this —

We watch them from way below,

Casting their music by the fields and sea —

All over, all over the suburbs.

Indeed, the moon being the centre claim of all,

Causing us to feel all joy and melancholy at once —

How graciously are they set up,

Oh, how graciously are they set up,

I ask myself.

I ask myself.

And when night falls,

I fall to the ground too,

Watching them take me paradise over paradise —

So endlessly, so beautifully.

I try to describe the moonlight endlessly,

Causing all inspiration to flow through,

I might be an artist,

But I had been a great lover first —

Yes, of nature, of nature.

How blessed is a person who gets to read beautiful heart-wrenching poems at his darkest moments in the darkest of hours lying on his bed where the moon light brims its shine onto him and having the stars on the lookout by the windowpane when the whole world is in deep slumber.

All you have to do is be there for yourself during both the shimmering times and the darkest of days. I tell you, down the line in probably two to five years, everything that is clouding you right now would simply turn into the tiniest dust that you could blow off if you like to. You wouldn't force yourself to forget things but, in fact, you simply wouldn't remember too much because everything that seeped in through you once eventually will find a way to seep out too. So, when everything is only gonna turn into dust a few years, why bother? When something is happening, relax, observe and gracefully choose. Under any circumstances, choosing you is the biggest gift you would provide yourself with. It's not wrong to choose you and think good of you. In fact, each one should think of themselves first and then provide as much as they can to the others around. I think if everybody knew how to genuinely take care of themselves, the world would be a less tangled place. But whatever — being your own person who you have always wished to have is the kindest thing you can do for yourself. Have a simple gentle relationship with yourself and place yourself in places where there is room for beauty and growth and you grow slowly and steadily at your own pace. So, make sure you bloom again not because you want to show you can bloom but because you have the capability to bloom. Again, nothing would matter, so you might as well not give a damn when something unexpected comes your way. Learn from the happenings — be it something unexpected or something that came up because of the consequences of your actions and discard them. Nothing's worth so much of your time that it steals your present and everything that you can make out of the moments waiting. So, you might as well choose things as you would for someone that truly matters, and that you'd truly stick with, for better or for worse. That is all that is needed.

And if you can endure the hardship and come out of something, you possess the ability to overcome many things, if not everything, and isn't that a good omen in itself, right?

It is almost funny that no matter what you do and how hard you work to get somewhere, there is always a bunch waiting to bring you down by managing to diminish everything you have done to precisely nothing. You know you have to somehow rise beyond the muffled voices, yet you don't know how to and that makes the process much difficult. If there is something that I have learnt or felt along the way, it is that the hard times are mostly caused by people to other people. They will simply walk over you like a dead leaflet if you fall down. Sometimes worst is that they would pluck you, push you off the ground and then walk over. Sometimes all you have to do is guard yourself from them — to get away from everything and everyone even if it means you standing alone. Sometimes all you need is some space. Nothing more, nothing less and just that.

Sometimes the shadows to heed are from people who bring us down.

The most beautiful thing, I suppose, is cherishing the honest, vulnerable truths about ourselves, unaltered by the opinions of others or the ways we got caught up in. We can always shed parts of ourselves we no longer desire, but not our innate truths—they are the traces of our roots. I've learned to understand that we all possess different truths, but how beautiful and courageous it is to find, understand, and have the courage not to eliminate them but to cherish and embellish them. Not necessarily to show or make others see our innate selves, but to hold onto them merrily for ourselves. How beautiful it is to really understand ourselves, all by ourselves, all for ourselves.

Each have their own truths. Your work is to find yours.

Things feel quite easy when you constantly remind yourself that the world doesn't revolve around you and that you are not perfect and that there isn't any need to be. It is rather beautiful to walk a step towards the mirage of perfection than running on bare feet towards it turning the very process unbearable. You don't have all the answers and you have time to figure it all and therefore you should stop putting yourself under constant pressure each moment. You are flawed and so are all. I think we all have the capability to try and change at any point. If there is one thing you wish to do for yourself, it is forgetting the notion of wanting to prove yourself to someone every damn time. You don't deserve such a lifelong imprisonment, do you? You let the minutes flow in pure harmony and live life. Don't battle naively. Don't struggle without reason. Drive out things that drive you off the shore. Appreciate everything in general and yourself in particular.

Let their thoughts be distant echoes

for their musings hold no sway

over your journey.

Working hard is commendable, but dedicating effort to the wrong pursuit won't bring fulfilment. To discern what's right, practice patience, heightened awareness, and consistent introspection. Give your all to endeavours yet be vigilant for the wildfire that consumes your soul. When you sense it burning, intervene, extinguish, and discard what doesn't resonate. Discovering what's wrong is witnessing your soul's decline, prompting you to take control and seek soul-satisfying endeavours. Learning accompanies burns; they guide you away from scorching experiences. This is a reliable path to self-discovery, isn't it?

If it alighted on your lap with the descent of the winds, would you deem it worthy? Conversely, if you sweated profusely and poured your all into something, would you cast it aside? Everything holds value; what's insignificant to you might be invaluable to another. Your task is to discern what you find worthy and let the rest stand undisturbed for others to embrace. It's a matter of handling things with beauty and grace, entirely within one's control.

YOU HAVE IT ALL. NEVER MEASURE YOURSELF LESS.
YOU ARE ALL YOU EVER NEED AND WILL ALWAYS HAVE!

~ Y.

www.ingramcontent.com/pod-product-compliance
Lightning Source LLC
LaVergne TN
LVHW091330150826
845673LV00006B/1822

* 9 7 9 8 8 9 1 3 3 7 0 3 9 *